The Messenger & the Skeptic

Karen Liptak

Illustrations by Jana Liptak

The Messenger & The Skeptic by Karen Liptak
Originally published in 2017 by Cosmic Light Publishing

All rights reserved. No part of this book may be reproduced or transmitted in any form or by any electronic or mechanical means, including photocopying, recording, or by any information storage and retrieval system, without the express written permission of the copyright holder, except where permitted by law. This novel is a work of fiction. Names, characters, places, and incidents are either the product of the author's imagination, or, if real, used fictitiously.

Trade Paperback ISBN: 979-8-9913238-0-2

Illustrations and figures are the property of Jana Liptak & Karen Liptak
Cover design by Cheryl Ryan @ https://cherylryan.com/
Cover art by https://photojournal.jpl.nasa.gov/catalog/PIA10967
Back cover image photo by Olena Bohovyk on Unsplash (https://unsplash.com/@olenkasergienko?utm_content=creditCopyText&utm_medium=referral&utm_source=unsplash)

Published by 3sides2 Author Services
P.O. Box 85161
Tucson, AZ 85754
Eva M. Eldridge, publisher
3sides2 Edition 2024
Printed in the USA

The Messenger & the Skeptic

A Message From the Author

Have you ever wondered if there's more to life than meets the human eye? If so, my books are for you.

The seeds for *The Messenger & The Skeptic* were planted on April 8, 1976. That's when I had a 'cosmic breakthrough; a sudden gust of wind roared *"Move on,"* and took me mentally from Manhattan to where I thought many things seemingly too impossible to be true! How could this world end? How could I learn to write for the next? And how could a loving, wise, and powerful force guide me to think from a cosmic perspective?

Fantastic thought after thought poured in. Yet they *felt* more real than the life I'd lived. Eventually, I reasoned that *just in case* this was more than my imagination, I should follow as led. Since then, I've spent decades evolving my writing to help me explain why I think two human species now exist on Earth. One species will naturally go extinct. The other will transition to a higher state of mind, in which to repair the planet, help each other reach their full potential, and connect with the cosmos.

In '76, I couldn't envision a guiding force pulling off changing the world. Nor could I imagine creating the critical mass of material needed to make my case. But as my writing improves, and scientists grow humbled by how little they know—only 5% of what exists—I've gained the confidence to share my journey. And while I can't prove what happened to me, where my writing stems from, nor how or when this world will transform, I offer my experience and *The Messenger & The Skeptic* as gifts to all who think there must be more to life than meets the human eye.

Karen

She said, *"I'm a messenger
of the cosmic kind."*
The Skeptic assumed
she was out of her mind.

Arrogant, too,
and annoying as hell,
swearing she'd come
with a message to tell.

Leery of phonies,
and honest to the bone,
The Skeptic trusted tests;
tests and tests alone.

So, with truth his objective,
he locked her in his cave,
a slew of tests on hand
to see how she'd behave.

His goal was to prove
by her actions and words
her claim no more real
than flying elephant birds.

AEPYORNITHIDAE
(Elephant Birds)

Flightless elephant birds were native to the island of Madagascar. They were believed to have been 10 feet tall and weighed close to 880 lbs. They became extinct in the 17th or 18th century.

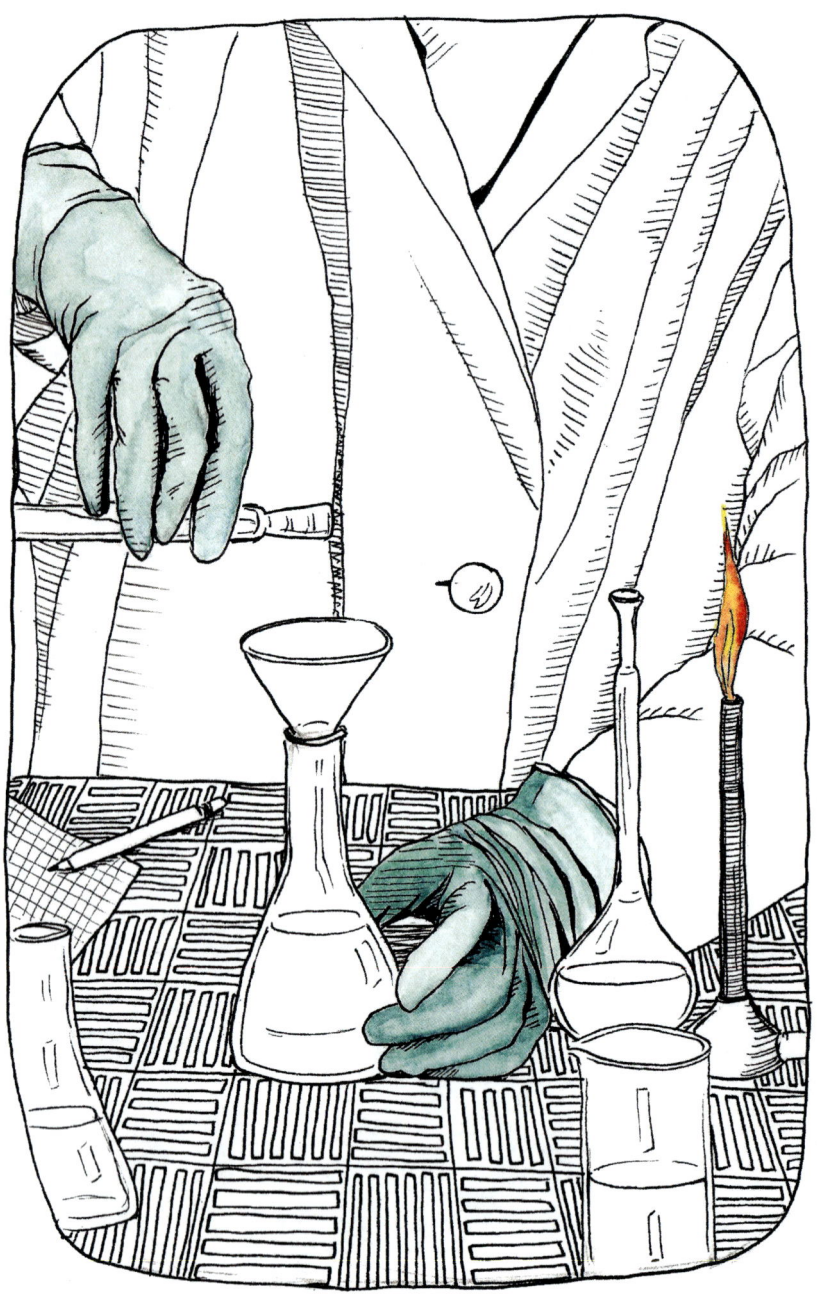

He got right to work
in his gloves and lab coat,
sure he'd soon have
the data to gloat.

He began with commands
in a growl worse than gruff,
and when she flinched, yelled,
"A messenger would be tough!"

He laughed at her visions,
called her a space head,
and whenever she spoke,
ridiculed all she said.

He forced her to sleep
on a mattress of straw,
and scrub every rock
on his cave's filthy floor.

He forbade her fresh water
when she wanted a bath,
and sneered at her offer
to help him do math.

He refused her a light
so that she could read,
snapping if asked,
like a turtle on speed.

When her birthday came,
all he gave her was grief.
He tried robbing her faith
like the world's biggest thief.

But whenever he checked
his Truth-Or-Fiction-O-Graph,
he didn't know whether
to cry or to laugh.

It clearly revealed
she was being sincere;
she'd come with a message
that he had to hear.

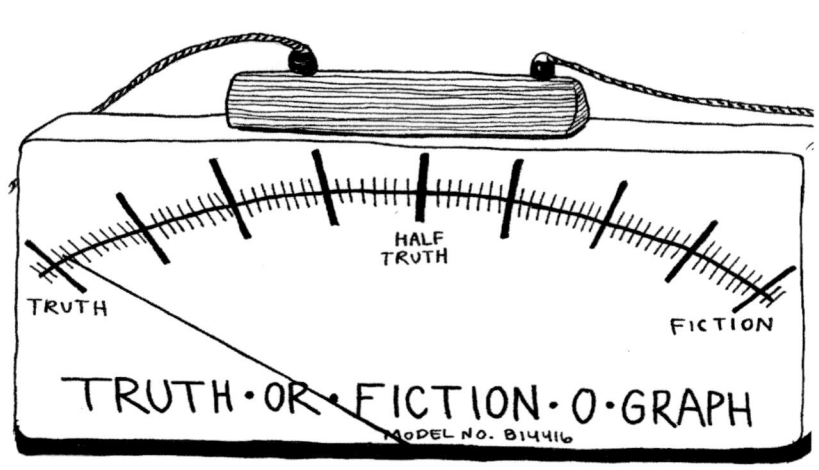

Refusing to think
he might not be right,
he slept not a wink,
running tests day and night.

"The truth is my God,"
he said time and again,
"and until you confess,
you're not leaving this pen."

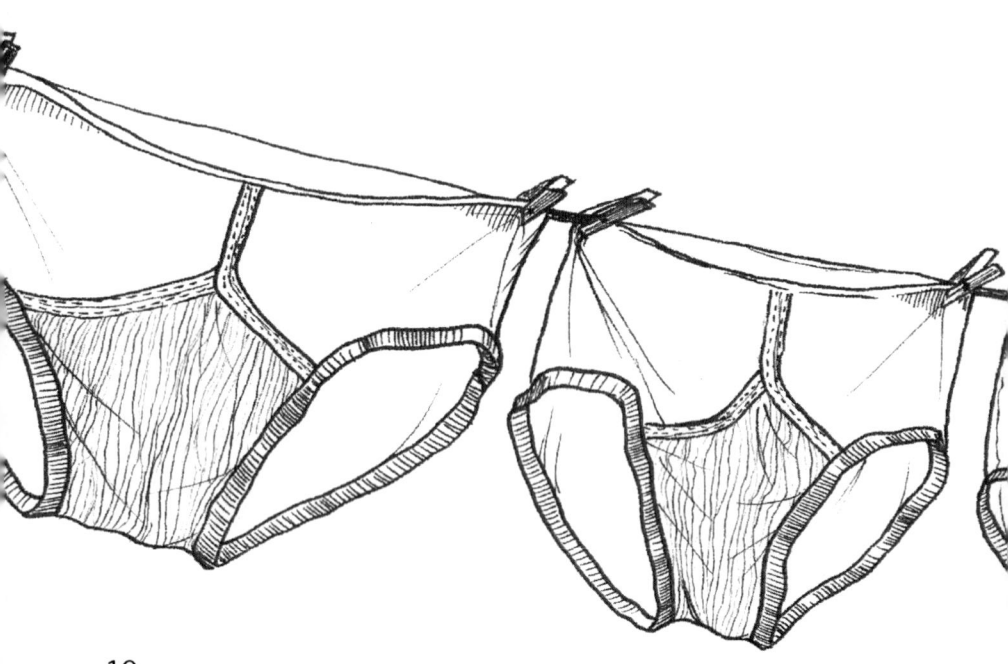

The more that she swore
in no way had she lied,
the more his blood boiled
and his tests multiplied.

He demanded she darn
his socks one by one,
then wash all his briefs,
and he had a ton.

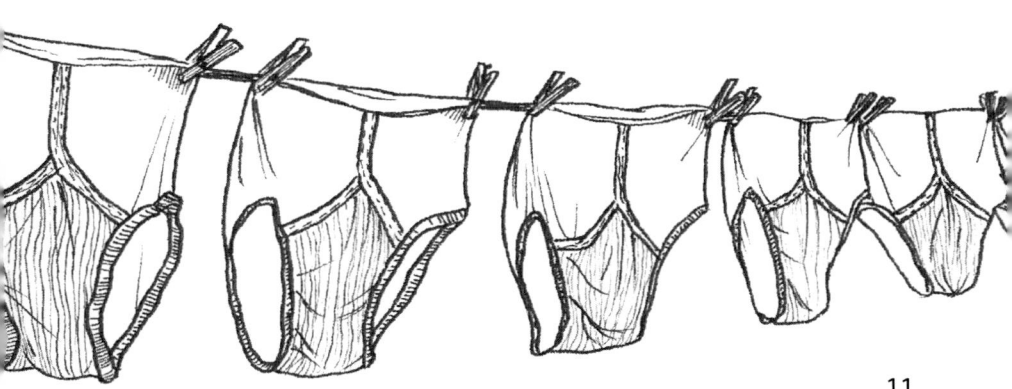

He belched in her face
like a drunk, sloppy lush,
and cursed with such rage,
a bar bouncer would blush.

He said she was ugly,
and looked twice her age.
He critiqued her writing as

Still, she wouldn't admit
she was really a fraud,
like so many humans are,
their thinking badly flawed.

Instead, she said, *"No test,
nor ear plugs, nor humming,
can shut out what I must say
about a new world coming."*

Her words, softly spoken,
fell on out-to-lunch ears,
while her wistful smile
repelled all his jeers.

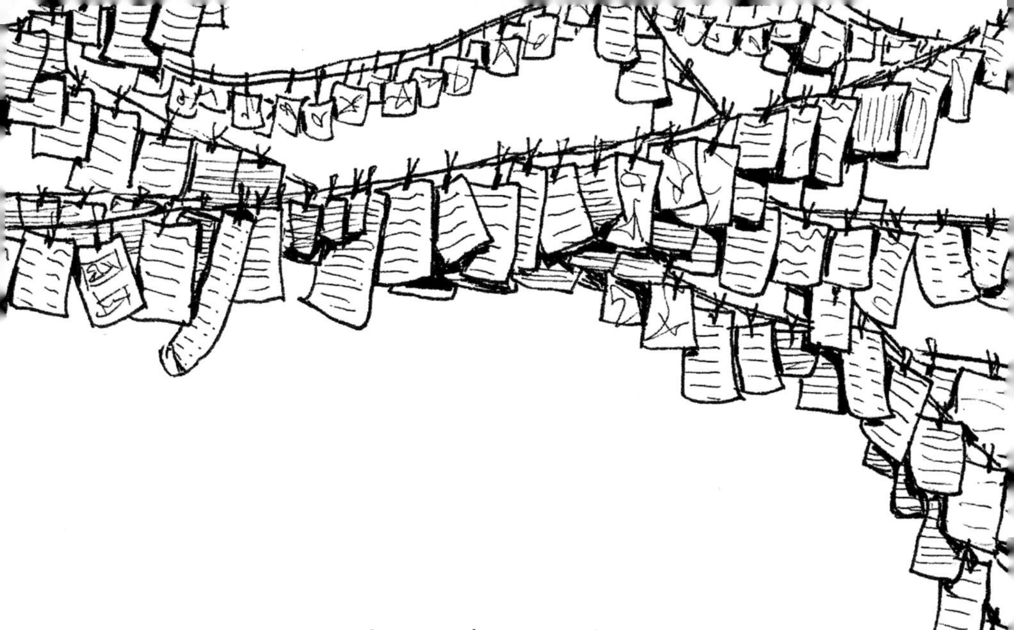

Aware he was hers
to secretly prime,
to begin a journey
at a predestined time,
she cut him much slack,
and she didn't plead nor nag,
though his notes by the trillions
caused his man cave to sag.

And she took it in stride
when he called her a fake.
"Cosmic messenger, you?
Please give me a break."

As a matter of fact,
he got a *break-through*,
once he could accept
how little he knew.
Each test that she aced
made his ego crack more,
till The Messenger sensed
his mind ripe to soar.

So, acting demure,
she asked to please bake
her cosmic crowd pleaser,
Deep Sky Angel Cake.

A sucker for sweets,
he agreed to her wish,
unaware all she planned
to put into the mix.

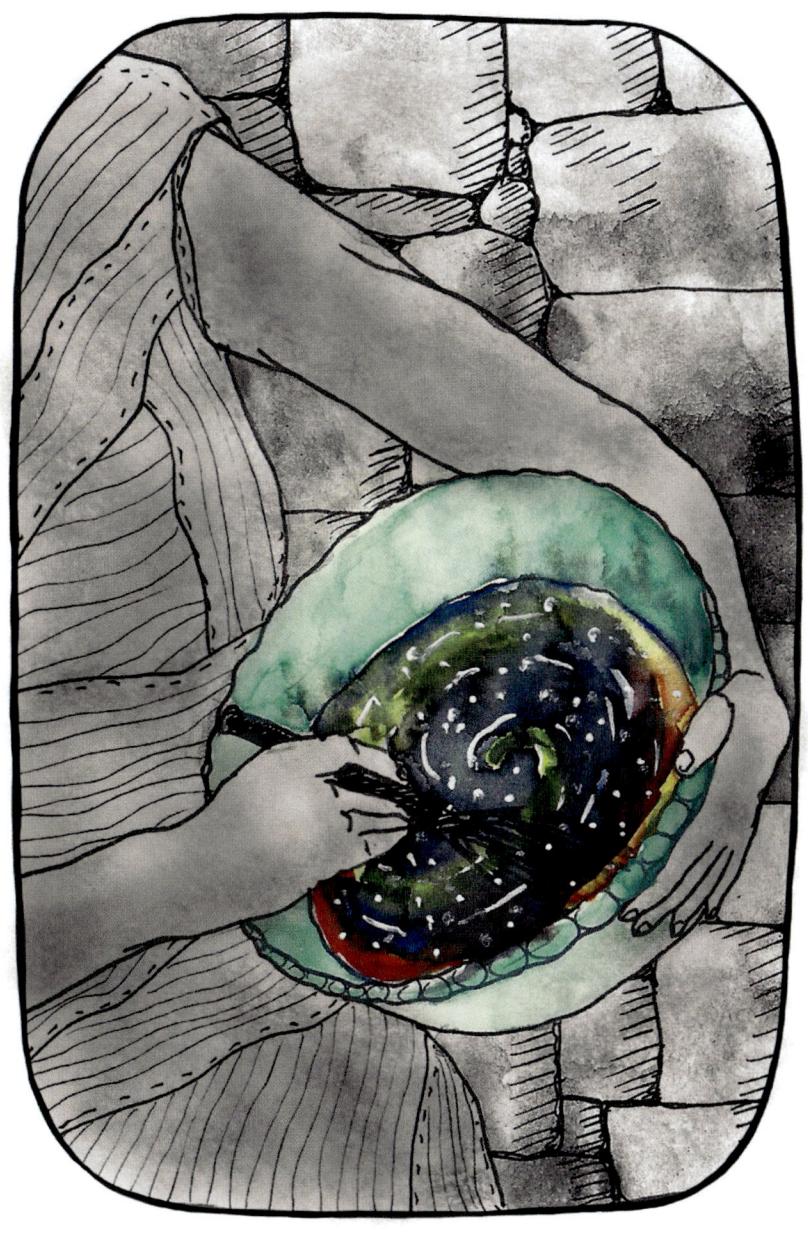

And while he went back
to do work and complain,
The Messenger prepped
to drive the man sane!

She loaded her batter
with much food for thought,
space missions nearing
answers long sought.

Then she sprinkled exoplanets,
their number beyond measure,
and signs of life elsewhere,
a spice to greatly treasure.

Next, a pinch of reasoning zest—
how humans ask, "Do aliens exist?"
while they themselves are tested
for cosmic contact readiness.

At last, cake in the oven,
The Skeptic sniffed his treat.
It sent a natural high
from his head to his feet.

And once her creation cooled,
The Messenger topped her cake
with rows of mystical candles,
as many as it would take.

Soon the candles blazed
mesmerizingly bright,
and The Skeptic, amazed,
in his mind found a light
that showed him a key
that led to a door
it fit perfectly.

With a leap of faith,
he opened that door,
to behold a new world
that he'd lived in before,
and instantly recall
he was one with all.

His brain racing
at a whirlwind pace,
The Skeptic felt dizzy,
and abundant grace.

Then, what he saw
made him gape in awe;
him a boy gazing at stars,
and children of tomorrow
seeing Earth from Mars.

He took his first bite.
He got a sudden jolt;
a thought as shocking
as a lightning bolt:

*Homo sapiens will become an ancient race,
Earthlings are needed to move on in space.*

There were just them two,
but he knew they weren't alone.
He cleared his throat and then said,
"It appears that very little is known.

"And that the life I've lived
was a fiction I dreamed,
with nothing the way
it once seemed to be."

Without further ado,
the scene turning surreal,
he set his lab notes aflame,
and felt himself start to heal.

Then, greatly humbled,
he asked his now guest,
*"How can I move on?
What must I do next?"*

"Breathe," said The Messenger,
her words clear and hushed.
*"Just go with the flow.
No need to feel rushed."*

Above their heads,
stars twinkled, *"Shalom,"*
and The Skeptic felt blessed
to be on the path home.

He knew he was ready
for a mental promised land,
where he'd learn cosmic thinking
in terms he'd understand.

The next move he made
brought The Messenger joy.
She watched a man kneel
where before stood a boy.

And reading his lips
she saw him give praise
for the cosmic energy nearing
to guide humanity's next phase,
the old world ending, the cosmos
sending thoughts for those tending
Earth's cherished young fruits,
so the future proceeds
with strong, sturdy roots.

The Skeptic marveled
as thoughts filled his brain
that Earthlings not yet born
will be the first to explain.

Meanwhile, message
delivered, mission done,
The Messenger wondered
if she might have some fun
before ordered to split,
elsewhere to appear,
other species to awaken,
other planets to repair.

A nanosecond later,
with unseen pokes,
the force known universally
for the wittiest cosmic jokes
made them turn to the east,
and what they saw in the sky
had them giggling like kids
as it went whooshing by.

Though skeptics insist
they're flightless and extinct,
this Elephant Bird waved,
then lovingly winked.

ABOUT THE AUTHOR

Karen Liptak is a native New Yorker, now living in Tucson, Arizona. She's authored many nonfiction books, mainly for children and young adults. These include *Out in the Night, Dating Dinosaurs and Other Old Things, Endangered Peoples,* and *Native American Sign Language.* She's also been a filmmaker, an editorial director, and a guide at Kitt Peak National Observatory, where she tried to make astronomy fun, and advised visitors to keep an open mind. Her current writing began on her Miracle Day in 1976, when a mysterious cosmic breakthrough started her on a journey to write with the hope that a cosmic perspective brings.

ABOUT THE ILLUSTRATOR

Jana Liptak is an illustrator, muralist, and scenic painter. She holds an MFA from Edinburgh College of Art and is a proud member of IATSE. Originally from Tucson, Arizona, Jana lives in Brooklyn, NY, with her partner and two young children.

Made in the USA
Coppell, TX
25 July 2025

52340098R00026